MANY OF US WON
the 23rd Psalm. We ma
means. Well, it's time t

has opened a new door with just one word. He invites you to read the Psalm and add the word, "when." When the Lord Is My Shepherd creates a timeless connection between King David's world and ours today. You will understand more clearly that David did not see God as somewhere out there, but he saw God as an intimate friend, as his personal shepherd, and with this book, you will too. Read Roseberry's words devotionally and you, too will see yourself as a person after "God's own heart."

Karen Moore/AUTHOR/SPEAKER
Strength for the Soul
It's Still Possible

A COUPLE YEARS AGO I committed to memorizing and praying the 23rd Psalm. In the morning it is a prompt for prayer. At night it is a guide to thanksgiving. When the Lord is My Shepherd by David Roseberry is a gift to us who want to live the life suggested in the Psalm. This is David at his best: an intelligent and creative communicator helping us see what we would not see on our own.

The Right Rev. Todd Hunter, BISHOP
Churches for the Sake of Others

WHEN THE LORD IS MY SHEPHERD is a timely book that will help you find hope and meaning in the midst of the uncertain times we are living in. You will find your faith renewed and refreshed in these short meditations on Psalm 23.

Dr. Winfield Bevins
DIRECTOR OF CHURCH PLANTING AT ASBURY SEMINARY
AUTHOR, *Simply Anglican*

EVERYTHING IN THIS PRAYER begins with one term—Shepherd, and one claim—The Lord is our shepherd. Once we learn that the Lord is our shepherd, our life finds its orientation, its peace, and its joy. A wonderful devotional for our troubled times.

Rev. Canon Dr. Scot McKnight
PROFESSOR OF NEW TESTAMENT
NORTHERN SEMINARY

DAVID ROSEBERRY has captured a fresh and invigorating picture of the 23rd Psalm and opens our eyes to see the Shepherd for who he really is. His words are not just to be read, but to be prayerfully read and digested into our lives. When the Lord is our Shepherd, infinite possibilities open up for the one who follows the Shepherd.

The Most Rev. Foley Beach
ARCHBISHOP, ANGLICAN CHURCH
IN NORTH AMERICA

THE BOOK IS OUTSTANDING, convicting and is helping me personally see Psalm 23 in a whole new light. I've been using these devotions while on vacation with the family. We have all loved it.

The Rev. Al Zadig
Rector, St. Michael's Church, Charleston

When
THE LORD
IS MY
SHEPHERD

FINDING HOPE IN A HARD TIME
23 READINGS ON THE 23RD PSALM

David H. Roseberry

ANGLICAN COMPASS

AN IMPRINT OF LEADERWORKS
PROSPER, TEXAS

WHEN THE LORD IS MY SHEPHERD:
Finding Hope in a Hard Time
© 2020 by David H. Roseberry

Scripture quotations marked ESV are from the ESV® Bible (The Holy Bible, English Standard Version®), copyright © 2001 by Crossway, a publishing ministry of Good News Publishers. Used by permission. All rights reserved.

ISBN
Paperback: 978-1-7343079-6-2
Ebook: 978-1-7343079-7-9

Text and Cover Design by Blu Design Concepts

1. 23rd Psalm 2. Devotions 3. Meditations 4. Christian Living

ANGLICAN COMPASS

An Imprint of LeaderWorks
1080 Firewheel Lane
Prosper, Texas 75078

AnglicanCompass.com

Published in the United States of America

For my daughter Taye
who is a blessing, a beauty,
a faithful follower of Jesus
and a work of art herself.

PREFACE

EARLY IN JANUARY of 2020, I began writing a series of devotional readings to be used in an annual program for my denomination. It was my intention to write a series of reflections and meditations on stewardship and generosity. I have a keen desire to help all believers in Christ and their churches understand the amazing power of generosity and stewardship.

I had a great theme and a catchy working title, but this book is not that. Why? Because two weeks after I started outlining the work I ran into a wall.

COVID-19. The Coronavirus. The Pandemic.

It changed everything. Oh, I had plenty of time to write— we all did! —but I struggled with what to say. I could not fathom what was happening around the world and in my country. Our political and medical leaders appeared on the television every day warning us of a cresting wave of sickness and death. The economy was at a standstill. Job losses were staggering. I grieved for all the families who were so terribly hurt by the novel coronavirus.

In my quiet times during the morning hours, as I tried to process and pray through the unfolding catastrophe, I happened to read Psalm 23. As the pandemic wore on, I found myself returning to it every day for comfort, clarity, and strength. I said it over and over in my mind and in my prayers. I know it well. It is one of the few Psalms I have memorized for quick playback when needed. But the more I repeated this poem of King David, the more it seemed to me that these well-known verses were more than beautiful lines from an ancient time. In the days of the pandemic, these verses seemed more like promises to me.

Every image, phrase, metaphor, and line pointed to something that was promised to us when we allow the Lord to be our Shepherd in our lives.

Then, our country seemed to boil over. Protests and demonstrations against police brutality surfaced the raw wounds of racism. That touched off a wave of violence and destruction. And again, I found myself remembering the words from David's signature Psalm.

There is a confidence in his famous words. There are great lessons for us in this very uncertain time.

And of course, as we engage with the Psalm, we can apply its truth and meaning in a personal way. Many readers are enduring difficult times…or know someone who is. Psalm 23 has a remarkable way of speaking into the personal pain, fear, and anxiety that many people feel. It has done that for me.

Psalm 23 is an ode to a confident faith. Confidence in God is the theme from the first words of the poem to the last line of it. In this time, for this season, for this day, we need to hear these words from the shepherd boy who became a king.

It is my hope and my prayer that you will find more strength and confidence for a personal, daily walk with Jesus Christ. He is not only the Shepherd, but the Good Shepherd.

David H. Roseberry
AUGUST 2020

INTRODUCTION

PSALM 23 IS ONE of the most beloved pieces of poetry in the world. Thousands of years old, it has been used by millions of people to help them be strong in faith and maintain hope through difficulties and times of darkness. It has been prayed and proclaimed on the battlefield; it has been whispered to dying people at the bedside. It is beautiful, memorable, "memorisable," and deeply meaningful.

Here is how one preacher described the Psalm:

> *It has charmed more griefs to rest than all the philosophy of the world. It has remanded to their dungeon more felon thoughts, more black doubts, more thieving sorrows, than there are sands on the seashore. It has comforted the noble host of the poor. It has sung courage to the army of the disappointed. It has poured balm and consolation into the heart of the sick, of captives in dungeons, of widows in their*

pinching griefs, of orphans in their loneliness. Dying soldiers have died easier as it was read to them; ghastly hospitals have been illuminated; it has visited the prisoner, and broken his chains, and, like Peter's angel, led him forth in imagination, and sung him back to his home again. It has made the dying Christian slave freer than his master, and consoled those whom, dying, he left behind mourning, not so much that he was gone, as because they were left behind, and could not go too. (Spurgeon)

The aim of this book is to provide a new look at a very old poem written by the ancient king of Israel, David. Familiarity may have caused you to overlook its daring promises and clear convictions. Given the ancient age of the poem, you might assume that its language, metaphors, and simplicity would not apply in these complex times. But it does. I assure you.

David in His Day

The life of King David has been told on film, in stories, in lore, and in sermons for thousands of years. His life is chronicled in the Bible beginning midway through the Book of First Samuel. He comes into the story in Chapter 16. For this series, I will not attempt to outline his entire life, but I will say something about this man whom I have come to know over decades of personal study and teaching from the Old Testament.

David is a deeply emotional and complex man. He is a flawed leader, like every leader in the Bible, save one. His life is filled with high moments of personal achievement and spiritual joy as well as low periods of debauchery and sin. He did it all.

Readers of Bible stories often scratch their heads at how broken and tragic some of its luminaries are. Abraham trades his wife for safety. Isaac becomes a foolish old man. Jacob is a sneak-thief. Ruth is a flirt, albeit faithful. Saul is mentally unstable. Elijah is a depressive introvert. On and on the stories go in the Bible showing us all the foibles of great men and women of faith. Indeed, if we take off our stained-glass lenses, these people all look a bit too human. And that appears to be the point. We read the pages of the Bible and we can find ourselves in them.

Put another way, the Bible authors *describe* human life. They do not always *prescribe* human behavior. The authors are sometimes lifting these men and women up to us as role models and examples of walking in faith. But when the spotlight begins to shine on their mistakes and missteps, the authors are not commending their lives to us. They are not all role models of the faith all the time. They are renegade sinners in need of restoration and redemption. As are we.

David is no exception. His actions and decisions make him a hero, but the arc of his life baffles us. It is tragic, and tragically common in our own day. David rises from obscurity because of his deep faith in God. He is 'a man after God's own heart' whose desire for God spills out for all to see. He has everything he needs—privilege and position like none other. But then he loses it all because his sexual desire proves overwhelming.

There is much about David to admire, but the relationship with Bathsheba is not one of them. David is revealed to us as a deeply flawed person and his actions precipitated the long decline of his kingdom.

Today, most people are still looking for heroes and examples of the best of human life. However, every hero and role model that we are given to admire by the media and the culture ultimately fails to live up to the ideal. Every generation, it seems, needs to learn the perils of the pedestal. Whoever is hoisted up for all to see, soon becomes the brunt of gossip and jokes that all will tell.

This is as human as it gets. If you read David's story of deception and deceit, it is terrible. He cannot be a hero to us. He was not the complete hero his people were looking for either. One day a hero would come...but not for 1000 years. Until then, the people of David's time would groan on. Their hopes for a redeemer and protector would remain unfulfilled. Indeed, after David betrays their hope, there is a gradual decline in faithfulness among the people of God until the time of Christ. Once again, as in ages before and ages since, people cried out for help. We still do.

David for Our Day

If King David were alive today, he could not relate to our life on many levels. He could not comprehend an electric light bulb. He would not understand what an automobile is or what it was for. An airplane would mystify him. But David could understand our fears of disease and death. David would understand what it means to be persecuted. He would understand what it means to lose a loved one. He could relate to our lives when we experience threats, danger, rejection, and betrayal. David would understand the challenges of being 'sheltered in place.' He actually was sheltered in his own city! He would also understand the tensions between adult children and their parents. He would certainly understand the temptations that plague us all. David would relate to our need to have a sense of purpose in life.

This is why we can turn to David in times like this. David can teach us about hope and confidence in God because of his own experience with Him.

As we look deeply into this man's signature poem and apply it to our lives, we will be changed. We need to find what David found in the hardest of the times he faced.

Reading this Book

To quote an old Anglican Collect (prayer), it is my hope that your reading of this short book will help you 'read, mark, learn, and inwardly digest' the words of Psalm 23. It is written to highlight the role of God as Shepherd in our lives; Jesus himself being our Good Shepherd. It is intended to help every reader find firm footing for their faith in the midst of uncertainty.

This book is a meditative guide to help people come to trust God and His love for them for the first time. If events in your life have made you wonder about God's love for you, I hope this book will lead you on a journey to regain your trust and confidence in the Lord.

You may choose to read one meditation each day, or you may read them all straight through. Regardless, I would encourage you to use this book as part of a daily pattern of prayer and reflection. Each short chapter begins with the Psalm (taken from the English Standard Version).

Read over the Psalm slowly every time you open this book—after all, what's your hurry? Read the Psalm out loud. Make this a habit and soon, you'll have memorized it. You will have hidden God's word in your heart.

This short poem is a treasure, and, in this study, we will closely attend to each shining gem, every word, every verse. I pray you will grow in the knowledge of God our Father through a careful examination of this Psalm. It could be that you will understand—as I have come to understand—that this poem is the perfect poem for our uncertain age.

While all Scripture is able to speak into our lives, the short verses of Psalm 23 find an easier path into our hearts and minds. It is so familiar. It is so beloved. It is so lovely and pastoral that we really want to know how to apply it in our lives.

About "When"

You will notice that I have inserted a single word in front of the Psalm beginning with the second reading below. I do not think that it detracts from the beauty of the poem. Rather, as I hope you will see, it adds rich, personal application for our lives. The poem is a statement of a faith, to be sure. But the addition of the single word "When" (in parenthesis) turns the psalm into something that we can take hold of. The word is like a 'handle' that allows us to carry the truth of David's psalm into our hearts, minds, and our lives.

Read the psalm. Read it as if for the first time. Read it slowly. Read it out loud. Take your time. Do not worry about going too deep with the poem too quickly. We will get there. And, by the time we complete this book, you will have memorized this Psalm.

(When) The Lord is my shepherd; I shall not want.

He makes me lie down in green pastures.

He leads me beside still waters.

He restores my soul.

He leads me in paths of righteousness

for his name's sake.

Even though I walk through the valley
of the shadow of death,

I will fear no evil,

for you are with me;

your rod and your staff,

they comfort me.

You prepare a table before me

in the presence of my enemies;

you anoint my head with oil;

my cup overflows.

Surely goodness and mercy shall follow me
all the days of my life,

and I shall dwell in the house of
the Lord forever.

1
The Psalm

THIS PSALM is only 6 verses long, 114 words in ESV version I will use in this book. Psalm 23 is a circle. It starts with the Lord and ends with the Lord, literally! The word Lord is mentioned only twice: once at the beginning of the first verse and then, at the end of the last verse, it comes back around to Lord. And within this 'circle' are some of the highest and most profound ideas and images we can think of; trust, love, suffering, peace, protection, soul, sin, righteousness, restoration, provision, and much more. These six verses are heavy, but they are also lofty, as we will see together.

Did you notice David is speaking first about God in the third person (He), and then near the end, he changes the voice of the poem and addresses the Lord (You)? Also, the speaker switches metaphors mid poem. The first metaphor is of a Shepherd in the early lines; then we switch to the idea of a homeowner at the end. David sees himself first as a sheep, and then as the welcome guest and friend of the eternal landlord.

This is an accurate outline of the spiritual journey for most people who are believers today. First, they start out knowing things about God. They discover His attributes from stories in the Bible. They hear a sermon about His love or His goodness. They talk to a friend who tells them of God's presence in their life. They know about God. They speak about Him in the third person.

Then, as the journey goes, they come to know Him. He no longer seems distant and detached. He is present. Knowledge of God has gone from objective to subjective. People feel His presence. They know Him. And as we come closer to Him in faith, or as He comes closer to us in love, we come to know Him at a deeper level. We had known about Him, but now we know Him personally. We can speak to Him in the familiar You.

If you and I were to meet and become friends, we might talk about our past and our present. We'd each have a firm hold on that, at least. But the future is unknown for both you and for me. We cannot know what tomorrow or the day after that will bring. We cannot truly know for certain even one thing about our future.

Except . . .

The end of the poem promises a very clear and certain picture of our future. If we have come to know about God (He) and also know Him personally as Lord (You), then David says that we will dwell in His house forever. We will be with Him forever. We will dwell together. That much we can know, for certain.

You can see why this poem has been a source of hope for millions of people along their own journey and ultimately in their departure from this world. When we see the world shifting and changing right before our eyes, it is easy to be afraid. Fear builds upon itself in the human heart and mind. It only takes a little bit of it to get our imaginations going to produce more and more of it. Fear begets fear.

David's Psalm gives us the promise of the Shepherd's presence in our lives, and our presence with the Lord for eternity.

Read the text one more time, only this time insert the word 'when' before the first verse. "When the Lord is my Shepherd . . ." (We will do this for every reading.)

This small change shifts our perspective on the poem's direction dramatically. It becomes personal. Suddenly, we see the poem as a series of promises and protections that are ours. . . . when the Lord is our Shepherd.

When the Lord is my Shepherd,

my life's end will be to know

God and glorify him forever.

(When) The Lord is my shepherd; I shall not want.

He makes me lie down in green pastures.

He leads me beside still waters.

He restores my soul.

He leads me in paths of righteousness
for his name's sake.

Even though I walk through the valley
of the shadow of death,

I will fear no evil,

for you are with me;

your rod and your staff,

they comfort me.

You prepare a table before me

in the presence of my enemies;

you anoint my head with oil;

my cup overflows.

Surely goodness and mercy shall follow me
all the days of my life,

and I shall dwell in the house of
the Lord forever.

2
A Shepherd

WITHOUT ANY APOLOGY or explanation, David says that the Lord is a Shepherd to him. And not just *like*—God *is* a Shepherd. David, above anyone else, would know what a shepherd does. David was a shepherd himself. We know from the details of his storied life that he was a good shepherd. He was the protector of his sheep and the defender of his flock. At one point, David boasts that he was able to defend his sheep by killing ferocious predators nearby. We know that he lived with his sheep. That is the way of the shepherd.

Being a shepherd was a poor man's position in the Bible. It was the lowest of duties. The shepherd was literally among the sheep all the time—24/7/365. There was never a time when a shepherd would leave his sheep. The sheep might wander off, but the shepherd never would. He would always be *with* them. If it was raining and they got wet, he got wet. If the sheep were cold, then the shepherd shivered too.

God does not shrink back from the image of the shepherd. In fact, Jesus embraced it for Himself. He even amplified it. He called *Himself* the Good Shepherd. The Good Shepherd *watches* over the flock. The Good Shepherd *knows* each of the sheep by name. The Good Shepherd *leads* His sheep. In one analogy, Jesus says that the shepherd's job is to guard the sheep in a holding pen by literally laying down his life for their safety. (All of these phrases and verses come from John 10.)

One commentator on Psalm 23 underscores the beauty and truth of this image:

> *David uses the most comprehensive and intimate metaphor yet encountered in the Psalms, preferring usually the more distant 'king' or 'deliverer', or the impersonal 'rock', 'shield', etc.; whereas the shepherd lives with his flock and is everything to it: guide, physician and protector.*(Kidner)

This is one of the most central truths of our Christian faith. We are called to honor the Lord God as the King of the Universe. He is "high and lifted up" as the Ruler of all things. We do well to call Him Lord and to worship Him. But we also know that God came down to be with us; He lived among us as the lowest of servants. God (in Christ) would care for us the way a shepherd would care for his own sheep.

The cornerstone of the Christian faith is the belief that God is seen and honored as both *beyond* us and *beside* us.

Many people easily accept the truth that there must be a God, a creator of all things. How else can you explain the beauty of the planet and the wonder of life? But people struggle in their faith when they consider that God became a man. He lowered Himself down from the high vaults of heaven and took on our likeness in order to serve and to give His life as a ransom for many. That God is 'out there' is easy to believe for some; that He was also 'down here' is much harder to believe for all. But He is both heavenly Lord and earthly Shepherd.

This great mystery is here in the first line of our Psalm. David declares that there is someone who stands over all time and space as a God of glory; and also stands with Him to guide and protect Him day by day. This God is SomeOne. He is SomeOne over all things. He is SomeOne near him. He is SomeOne who knows his deeds and his needs. He is SomeOne who can care for the sheep as if they were His own children.

When the Lord is my Shepherd,
the God who is beyond me
is also beside me.

(When) The Lord is my shepherd; I shall not want.

He makes me lie down in green pastures.

He leads me beside still waters.

He restores my soul.

He leads me in paths of righteousness
for his name's sake.

Even though I walk through the valley
of the shadow of death,

I will fear no evil,

for you are with me;

your rod and your staff,

they comfort me.

You prepare a table before me

in the presence of my enemies;

you anoint my head with oil;

my cup overflows.

Surely goodness and mercy shall follow me
all the days of my life,

and I shall dwell in the house of
the Lord forever.

3
My Shepherd

BELIEVING THAT THE LORD is a shepherd is a pastoral idea. The functions and activities of our heavenly God are easier understood using a metaphor. But David takes it one step further. He says that the Lord is his shepherd. Now it's personal.

In the ancient world, 'the gods' were 'out there.' They inhabited the heavens or places beyond our view. They looked down from above. They were not personal at all. In fact, they were thought to ignore humans unless they were amused or until they were called upon. There was not just one God. There were many gods.

So, when the God of the Bible is declared to be the only God, it was a shock to the polytheistic nations around them. Further, the God of the Bible was declared not only to be the God of Israel, but the God of Abraham, Isaac, and Jacob. He was the God not only of a people (Israel) but of all persons. He is a personal God.

When David declares that the Lord is his Shepherd, he is saying that He is a personal God. He is also saying that He is personally knowable. The God of the Universe is not just the cosmic force that exists over and above all things. He is a personal God who knows our every thought and our every move.

We talk today about someone having a 'personal relationship with Jesus Christ.' When we hear that or say it ourselves, we should remember that personal does not mean customized. A personal relationship with Jesus does not mean that we get to pick only those directions or aspects of the Christian life that make us feel comfortable. No. A personal relationship with Jesus Christ is a matter of the heart. It is a matter of knowing, deep within, that there is a God who loves you, who came to save you, and who now lives beside you, and this God wants to direct and guide you.

Can you say out loud what David says here? The Lord is my Shepherd. These words are the beginning of fellowship with the God of the Universe. By saying "The Lord is my Shepherd," you have opened up your heart and your life to the influence, guidance, friendship, and protection of a loving God.

This simple early phrase in the Psalm is one of the most profound statements of faith and conviction that we can ever utter. It is a window into David's heart. He wanted his day-to-day life to reflect this. He did not always live up to this declaration. Neither do we. But it was his hope, as it is ours.

When the Lord is my Shepherd,
I will trust Him for everything.

(When) The Lord is my shepherd; I shall not want.

He makes me lie down in green pastures.

He leads me beside still waters.

He restores my soul.

He leads me in paths of righteousness
for his name's sake.

Even though I walk through the valley
of the shadow of death,

I will fear no evil,

for you are with me;

your rod and your staff,

they comfort me.

You prepare a table before me

in the presence of my enemies;

you anoint my head with oil;

my cup overflows.

Surely goodness and mercy shall follow me
all the days of my life,

and I shall dwell in the house of
the Lord forever.

4

I Shall Not Want

CAN YOU IMAGINE singing Psalm 23? The word Psalm is very much like our word song. These verses are lyrics, text for singing. It was for praise and worship; it was for truth and instruction. Many Psalms are written for the congregation to sing.

We are sure David did...and the first line of the song declared something amazing. The Lord is my Shepherd, I shall not want. It is a strong statement. It is a bold statement. It occurs as early in the Psalm as it can, and most people who attempt to recite this poem by heart know this short phrase.

But do we understand the magnitude of this little phrase? It is one of the strongest statements of faith that we can imagine. I shall not want!

What does the poet mean? I think there are two areas that can be explored here. First, David means that because he has recognized the Lord in the role of a shepherd over his life, he knows he will lack for nothing.

He trusts God. And he trusts God to go with him everywhere and to provide what is needed every time. He has confidence that he will always have more than enough. He has hope that whatever happens to him as his life unfolds (and a lot would happen to him), he would always know that God would provide for him.

We should be careful about what we think is meant by this. Some have perverted this promise of provision into a promise of prosperity. David surely didn't mean it this way. David is not saying that God has a supply chain of goodies direct from heaven for those who have faith. God did NOT provide for David that way all the time. There were times when he was in danger, fear, thirst, or deprivation. Even then, he had enough.

But second, the statement, "I shall not want" means something else; it means something more. He means that when the Lord is the Shepherd of my life, a quiet conversion begins to take place. The worldly things we have always wanted, begin to loosen their grip. We really do begin to think and feel differently about the things we want. A wise pastor once said that when a person comes to faith in God through His Son Jesus

Christ, the new convert's 'wanter' begins to change.

It is true. The conversion of the 'wanter' begins however slowly, but little by little we experience something we have been looking for our whole life. We have 'contentment.' We are no longer in want.

David is not saying that a loving God will deliver to us all the material wants we can imagine. There's no end to those. King David is not promising financial and material blessings, although those might come. "I shall not want" means I shall have something that eludes most people today. I shall have contentment, security, fellowship with God, and that is enough.

When the Lord is my shepherd,
I always have enough.

(When) The Lord is my shepherd; I shall not want.

He makes me lie down in green pastures.

He leads me beside still waters.

He restores my soul.

He leads me in paths of righteousness

for his name's sake.

Even though I walk through the valley
of the shadow of death,

I will fear no evil,

for you are with me;

your rod and your staff,

they comfort me.

You prepare a table before me

in the presence of my enemies;

you anoint my head with oil;

my cup overflows.

Surely goodness and mercy shall follow me
all the days of my life,

and I shall dwell in the house of
the Lord forever.

5

Lying Down

AT FIRST GLANCE, the second verse of the 23rd Psalm might distract you from the true meaning of it. "*He makes me lie down in green pastures.*" We can easily picture the intended reference of this short phrase…. beautiful, lush, green, fertile grasslands with shade trees and a flowing river come to mind. We might imagine little white dots of sheep scattered across the field munching on succulent grass. They are well-fed. It is a blissful, beautiful scene.

Indeed, in the Middle East, there are remarkably green pastures. It is not just the desert image we might have in our minds from Sunday School. There are breathtakingly beautiful green fields in the Jezreel Valley, but the hope of greener pastures is not the point of this second line in the Psalm. The surprising truth about David's statement is not that there are pastures or even that they are green. What is remarkable about this verse is that the shepherd has convinced the sheep to lie down!

Sheep are very skittish animals. They are totally aware of their surroundings; they always sense danger. They know how vulnerable they are, but here they are invited to lie down.

In the book, *A Shepherd Looks at Psalm 23,* by W. Philip Keller, we catch a glimpse of a real shepherd with a flock. Since he was a real shepherd, his insights into the characteristics of these sheep are classic. When he considers this verse, Keller says that sheep are so naturally nervous and worried they will not lie down to rest unless certain requirements are met. To get them to relax, the sheep need to have freedom from fear. That seems reasonable, but he also says they must be at peace with each other. They must have "freedom from friction" with other sheep. Plus, they require minimal aggravation from bugs and ticks and other kinds of nuisances in their life. Finally, they need to be well-fed, freedom from hunger. If these four conditions are met, they will lie down in peace.

If you are a believing Christian, you can read yourself into these four requirements. They represent the changes that happened in your life and heart when you received the Lord Jesus as your Savior. If you are not a Christian, these four requirements are four promises that God will make to you as you accept His Son, Jesus Christ.

When the Lord is your Shepherd, you can…

1. Release your fears and worries of this world. You find peace.

2. Forgive one another and make amends or, in some cases, ask for forgiveness from others. You will find yourself actually praying for your enemies.

3. Be free of those things that truly *bug* you: shame, guilt, resentment, or regret. You can end the guilt-trips and shame cycles you may inflict on yourself.

4. Experience a life of fullness and satisfaction that the world cannot give.

Christianity is not a religion of moral rules and accomplishments. There are rules and ways that encourage every believer to put their faith into action; to have a ministry or to exercise their gifts. But that is not the essence of the faith. The Christian is given the gift of the Holy Spirit when he or she comes to faith. The Holy Spirit begins to work inside the believer. Sometimes it happens quickly, and many fears and resentments are lifted all at once. Sometimes things that *bug* us might take time to heal. We might need counseling, correction, or prayer. But in every case, the work that must take place in a believer's life and heart is initiated and accomplished by the work of the Holy Spirit of God.

It happens in God's time. When it happens, we can relax and 'lie down'; we have peace.

When the Lord is my Shepherd,
I will find peace; I can relax.

(When) The Lord is my shepherd; I shall not want.

He makes me lie down in green pastures.

He leads me beside still waters.

He restores my soul.

He leads me in paths of righteousness
for his name's sake.

Even though I walk through the valley
of the shadow of death,

I will fear no evil,

for you are with me;

your rod and your staff,

they comfort me.

You prepare a table before me

in the presence of my enemies;

you anoint my head with oil;

my cup overflows.

Surely goodness and mercy shall follow me
all the days of my life,

and I shall dwell in the house of
the Lord forever.

6

Water

PSALM 23 BRINGS US to 'still waters' or 'quiet waters.' Commentators often point out that sheep require still (not moving) water; they do not drink from running brooks. That is interesting but it is not what should attract our attention. David is saying when the Lord is our Shepherd refreshment and satisfaction will be at hand. It will be right beside us.

It's there. However, we must be willing to drink.

Your parents might have told you this old truism: "You can lead a horse to water, but you can't make him drink." That is true because horses will only drink water when they are ready to do so. Even when water is available to horses, sheep, or even people, there is a very personal action that needs to take place to quench the thirst. One must drink and swallow. In order to satisfy the thirst of the sheep, the sheep must drink.

A long time ago in a desert in Samaria, Jesus met with a woman who was thirsty. She stood by a famous well outside her village in the heat of the day. She was there to find cool, refreshing water from a deep well. But when Jesus spoke to her, He found that she was also a deep thinker. She thought theologically. She knew the current religious debates and arguments about where God could be found and worshipped. Jesus acknowledged her spiritual quest. But then He addressed the deep longings that she had in her heart and soul. We find out that her sins were many and her shame was debilitating. Sure, she was thirsty, but she was also thirsting for something more.

In one of the most lovely and well-known encounters in the New Testament, Jesus met her at the deep well and He met her deepest longing too. He asked her to give him some water. We assume she did. Then she asked Him to give her His kind of water, *living water.* Of course, He does.

She draws, and He drinks; then He draws, and she drinks. Beautiful.

If you have ever been thirsty, you know you cannot think about anything else other than your thirst. It is a need that will not go away. You might be able to forget about it for a short while, but very soon, the deep desire for water will return. Your thirst is a serious problem that will only go away when you drink water.

David, the boy shepherd, must have known the local watering holes. Even in the desert, there are pools of water that make life sustainable. David's poem reveals to us that the Lord God provided for him at the most basic of all levels. He has given David water. He has led the poet to places of instant and deep refreshment.

This is the power of water. It will quench a thirst like nothing else. Instantly! Surely Jesus had this idea in mind when He went to Samaria and spoke with the woman at the well. We know He had same idea about thirst in mind when He went to Jerusalem in the middle of one of the highly trafficked Holy days. He stood in the marketplace near the Temple where people were coming and going according to their religious traditions. He waited until the end of the festival and then cried out at the top of his lungs the call from the Prophet Isaiah, "If anyone is thirsty, let him come to the water, let him come to Me, the true and living water. And when he does, a spring of water will burst forth in him that will well up for all eternity." (Isaiah 55)

The Gospel writer includes one important detail: Jesus waited until *the end* of the religious feast before He spoke. He didn't say a word during the rituals, protocols, and scheduled observances. But after everyone had done everything that could be done; after they had had their fill of all traditional religious ceremonialism, then Jesus spoke up. He cried out that anyone who was still thirsting for more could find it in Him. The old tired rituals were void; they did not meet the deep spiritual longing that everyone had. But Jesus does. He promised Himself as the Living Water so that we would never thirst again.

When the Lord is my Shepherd,
I will never thirst

(When) The Lord is my shepherd; I shall not want.

He makes me lie down in green pastures.

He leads me beside still waters.

He restores my soul.

He leads me in paths of righteousness
for his name's sake.

Even though I walk through the valley
of the shadow of death,

I will fear no evil,

for you are with me;

your rod and your staff,

they comfort me.

You prepare a table before me

in the presence of my enemies;

you anoint my head with oil;

my cup overflows.

Surely goodness and mercy shall follow me
all the days of my life,

and I shall dwell in the house of
the Lord forever.

7

My Soul

THIS IS THE SHORTEST single sentence of this Psalm. *He restores my soul.* It is an abrupt change from the previous images of green pastures and still waters. Those images were all about the ancient Middle Eastern world of sheep and grassy lands. But now we are at a whole new level. We have gone from metaphorical to metaphysical!

We know that we have a soul. We may not know how to define it, but the Bible does. A soul is what makes a human being alive to God. The first story of the Bible tells us that God 'breathed' His breath into the nostrils of the first man and he became a living creature. The soulless man looked like a man before, but it was the 'Breath of God' that made him alive. In the language of the Bible, the man received a soul. The King James Version of that same story (Genesis 2) says that the man becomes a living soul.

The bottom line is this: You have a soul. You are not just a robot with intelligence. You are not a material being…only. Nor are you simply the highest animal in the created order. There is another element within you that makes you unique from all types of life. You have a soul.

But, for all of us, there is something really wrong with our soul; something wrong *in* our soul. It is bruised. It is damaged. That is why it needs to be restored, as the Psalm says.

But here is an important truth to consider. Even though sins have hurt our soul, they didn't cause the damage to our soul initially. The damage in our soul is part of a nature that was passed on to us from our first parents in the Garden.

The Bible tells the story about the fall of humanity. We all know there is something to it no matter how we see the story, literally or spiritually. Something in us is not right. We know we are not right with ourselves. We often fall short of even our own expectations. We know there is something not right about our relationships with others. The countless wars that humanity has waged over the centuries prove that this brokenness is endemic to the human soul.

We also know, there is something wrong with our relationship with God. That is the most serious of all. This is the spiritual problem every human being faces, but there is a biblical solution to this problem. It is the main theme of the entire Scripture. In fact, if you want to sum up the Bible's story about our human lives in as few words as possible, this is a great place to start: *He restores my soul.*

David says that when the Lord is your Shepherd, He will restore your soul. David is making a promise that only God can keep. He says that when the Lord is our Shepherd … that deep part of us that makes us human is actually spiritually restored. When the Lord is our Shepherd, our broken or bruised or neglected soul is made alive in God.

When the Lord is my Shepherd,
He restores my soul.

(When) The Lord is my shepherd; I shall not want.

He makes me lie down in green pastures.

He leads me beside still waters.

He restores my soul.

He leads me in paths of righteousness
for his name's sake.

Even though I walk through the valley
of the shadow of death,

I will fear no evil,

for you are with me;

your rod and your staff,

they comfort me.

You prepare a table before me

in the presence of my enemies;

you anoint my head with oil;

my cup overflows.

Surely goodness and mercy shall follow me
all the days of my life,

and I shall dwell in the house of
the Lord forever.

8

Restoration

HAVE YOU EVER BEEN in a room as someone dies? Have you held the hand of a loved one who has literally 'passed away' or expired before your eyes?

From my experiences with these sorrowful moments, I can say that when a person expires, there is a definite change in the room. Before the last breath, there may be two or three people standing around the bedside singing or praying or weeping. When that person dies, there is one less person. Someone has left the room. It is unmistakable. A soul is gone.

We have a soul. It is true that we have strong genetic instincts, natural appetites, primitive passions, and raw reactions that sometimes lead us into trouble; they always lurk below the surface of daily lives. But we are much more than that. We are much more than our genes! Dallas Willard reminds us of the dignity of our human nature when he writes: "You are a never-ceasing spiritual being with an eternal destiny in God's great universe."

As mentioned, in this short sentence of Psalm 23, the poet David shows us that we have a soul, a spiritual being that is part of our nature. If we live only by what we can see and measure, we will miss the bigger picture. We have a soul.

The physical promises offered to the sheep (still waters and green pastures) are alluring images. But the real need is for the restoration of the soul.

Who can do this restoration project? Who can restore our soul?

You see, the Bible's remedy for this broken world and our broken relationships is to come into them and heal them all. The Gospel story tells us this over and over again. Christ came into the world to save sinners. He came to seek and save the lost. He is the Good Shepherd who seeks the lost sheep. He calls His sheep by name. He lays down His life for the sheep.

David lived a hard life. As a King, you might think he had all the privileges of a regal position. He did, for a time. But he was hunted by those who wanted him dead; he was haunted by the memory of those who were dead: his unnamed baby, Uriah his friend, Jonathan his best friend, and Absalom his grown son. More than once in his poetry, he talks about the weariness of his soul.

The Shepherd restores our souls. He gives us rest. Or at least, Jesus wants to. Remember the loving way He phrased it as He looked over the crowds, and His heart was moved for them. He said they were like sheep without a shepherd. As a Shepherd, He called them to come to Him. "Come to me all who are heavy laden and burdened and I will give you rest."

This is the way the restoration process begins. To paraphrase James 4:8, we take a step toward Him; then He takes a step toward us.

When the Lord is my Shepherd, my restoration is through Jesus Christ.

(When) The Lord is my shepherd; I shall not want.

He makes me lie down in green pastures.

He leads me beside still waters.

He restores my soul.

He leads me in paths of righteousness

for his name's sake.

Even though I walk through the valley
of the shadow of death,

I will fear no evil,

for you are with me;

your rod and your staff,

they comfort me.

You prepare a table before me

in the presence of my enemies;

you anoint my head with oil;

my cup overflows.

Surely goodness and mercy shall follow me
all the days of my life,

and I shall dwell in the house of
the Lord forever.

9

Leading Me

"THEY ARE NOT GOING ANYWHERE!" She was speaking about the flock of sheep across the ravine at the Wadi Qelt in Israel. This canyon is one of the most spectacular vistas in all of Israel. I have led dozens of groups there and it is always impressive: the centuries-old monastery is hanging on the far canyon wall; the ravine plunges down 250 feet to a narrow creek of water. It is here that the sun is reported never to shine into the canyon. It is that deep and narrow. On the bluffs of the canyon wall are small flocks of sheep nibbling on the grass in the rainy season. The lady who spoke to me about the flocks was noticing how still they were. Indeed, they didn't seem to be going anywhere.

Yes, it is true. The small flocks of sheep simply 'hang out' munching on the available vegetation. They seem to be headed nowhere. Aimless. They are pointing in all different directions, moving this way and that. The shepherd doesn't appear to lead them or to follow after them. He is just standing around in the midst of them.

I told her that we should keep an eye on the flock since it was near the end of the day and the flocks would be moving toward their sheep pen. As the sun began to set, the flock moved slowly and deliberately. The shepherd boy who had stood in the middle of the flock simply began to make his way home, to shelter and safety. The sheep began to follow. Wherever the boy led, the sheep followed.

The Psalm tells us that the shepherd leads the sheep. Leading the sheep is the most common of all shepherd practices, I'd imagine. Jesus says as much in His discourse of the Good Shepherd (John 10). Where He leads, the sheep follow.

Following Jesus, our Shepherd, is the goal of the Christian walk of faith. It is not to get every point of doctrine correctly all the time. It is not to convince others of the truth of the Gospel. The goal of the Christian life is not to 'make it to heaven.'

It seems to me, from the life of Jesus and the words of this Psalm, that the goal of the Christian life is to follow Christ; to acknowledge Him as our Shepherd and, in faith, follow Him as Lord.

There is a vivid scene in Herman Melville's classic *Moby Dick*. You may know the story. Early on in the novel, the narrator, Ishmael, goes to church before he launches out on the fabled voyage. The sermon that is preached to the assembled congregation is all about our reluctance to obey God. The text Fr. Mapple preaches is appropriately from the Book of Jonah. The fictional preacher proclaims a truth about obedience that is as true as it is difficult to hear, "If we are to obey God, we must first disobey ourselves. It is in disobeying ourselves that the hardness of obeying God exists."

The challenge for any Christian is not only to believe in Jesus. That, as it turns out, is the easy part. The hard part is to believe Him and follow Him where He leads because it usually means that we must disobey ourselves.

When the Lord is my Shepherd,
I know that he will lead me.

(When) The Lord is my shepherd; I shall not want.

He makes me lie down in green pastures.

He leads me beside still waters.

He restores my soul.

He leads me in paths of righteousness
for his name's sake.

Even though I walk through the valley
of the shadow of death,

I will fear no evil,

for you are with me;

your rod and your staff,

they comfort me.

You prepare a table before me

in the presence of my enemies;

you anoint my head with oil;

my cup overflows.

Surely goodness and mercy shall follow me
all the days of my life,

and I shall dwell in the house of
the Lord forever.

10

The Path of Righteousness

THE PATHS OF RIGHTEOUSNESS is an interesting blending of words and worlds. A path is something we use to go from place to place. It is a worn-out area in the ground that leads somewhere, and the Psalm tells us that the path leads to righteousness. *Righteousness* is one of the most consequential words in the Bible. It means to be in a right relationship with God, and it is something that God confers upon us.

In this short sentence from Psalm 23, the poet is telling us that the shepherd will lead us into a pathway where the outcome will be a right relationship with God.

Think of it this way: there is a path on which we can travel to a place where we can be in a right relationship with God. There is a path that leads to a holy place; there is a way that leads to a place of righteousness.

Remember the biblical story of Abraham? In one of the most remarkable meetings in history, Abram is given a promise by God. Abram could rely upon God to produce an heir for him and for his descendants. God has called Abram to leave everything behind and follow to a place as yet unknown to him, and Abram did that. He packed up everything and left on this journey. But somewhere along the way, it got confusing. Mistakes were made. Faithlessness edged out faithfulness. Abram is looking for some reassurance that he has not lived his life in vain. He wants to be assured that God is still sure about him; that all of His promises will still apply to him even though he is an old, old man.

God tells him again that he will be the father of many nations. There will be an heir to the throne even though there is not even a throne! God assures Abram that he can rely on Him. And somehow, Abram believed Him. When Abram believed God, it was accounted to him as righteousness. It is as if God said to Abram, "You don't have to worry about anything after what you just said. You have come to believe and when you come to believe you have arrived!"

The Psalm gives us the same assurance. There is a path

where we can be led. And when we embark upon that path, when we are led, it is enough. It brings us into a right relationship with God.

This is the point of one of Jesus' most famous sayings in John 14. Jesus told His disciples that He was going to a place where He would prepare a place for them and then He would come back and lead them to it. Thomas asks, "Lord, we do not know where you are going. How can we know the way?" In the language of Psalm 23, Thomas was saying that he did not know the path. Jesus answered him, *I am the path.*

Psalm 23 reminds us that there is a path in front of us where Jesus leads us into a right relationship with God. And He Himself is the path.

When the Lord is my Shepherd, I am led into a right relationship with God.

(When) The Lord is my shepherd; I shall not want.

He makes me lie down in green pastures.

He leads me beside still waters.

He restores my soul.

He leads me in paths of righteousness
for his name's sake.

Even though I walk through the valley
of the shadow of death,

I will fear no evil,

for you are with me;

your rod and your staff,

they comfort me.

You prepare a table before me

in the presence of my enemies;

you anoint my head with oil;

my cup overflows.

Surely goodness and mercy shall follow me
all the days of my life,

and I shall dwell in the house of
the Lord forever.

11

His Name's Sake

SO FAR, THE PSALM has focused on all the things that the Shepherd provides for the sheep. God's provision, restoration, peace, safety, and satisfaction are all things that the Shepherd gives to the sheep. It is a completely one-sided arrangement. The sheep merely receive. God is the giver of all of this goodness.

Now we find out why. Why does God provide like this? What are his motives? What is behind it? David knows the answer because he knows God.

Often when we read the Bible, we have ourselves in mind. We are looking for good guidance or understanding. We might be looking for comfort or direction through a difficult time. Indeed, we will find much guidance and hope there. That might make us think the Bible is really a book about our life and times, a book about us.

That is partly true. A Bible reader cannot help but see herself in the text. She opens the book, finds the words, reads them slowly, and then takes them to heart. She feels she has discovered an ancient mirror, and in a way, she has.

But the main subject of the Bible is not you or me. It is God. God is the principal character. He is the storyline. He is the storyteller. The Word of God is about God. You may say that it was written for us, but the Bible is about our Triune God.

This is why it would make sense, as David tells us, that God would give these amazing things to us for His Name's sake. He has done all the things mentioned in the Psalm in order to increase the power, influence, and strength of His name. That is what 'for His Name's sake' means.

We have a hard time understanding this. It sounds like God is good because He wants widespread, eternal bragging rights. Is He a cosmic narcissist? Of course not! But how are we to understand that He does all of this goodness for His Name's sake, or better understood, 'for the sake of His Name'?

Think of the King of a realm. The King's role is to govern and rule over the land with justice and mercy. He has oversight and total responsibility for the protection of the people and the stewardship of the land. As long as the King is on his throne, the land will prosper. Subjects of the King can live their lives, enjoy their families, work to increase their wealth and health. People live their lives in thankfulness and service because of the King. He is their King and their life is good. Everything flourishes if everyone knows that the King is the King of all.

The reason why God, the King would want His name known and lifted high among all people is not for the bragging rights for all generations. He loves the people. He wants His name known for the flourishing of the people and the land. As long as everyone knows that the King is enthroned, all will be well.

David gives the reason why his Shepherd has given him these things. It is for the sake of His name and for the benefit and flourishing of His people. In other words, God gives for the sake of His Name for the sake of His people.

When the Lord is my Shepherd, I discover that His glory is for my own good.

(When) The Lord is my shepherd; I shall not want.

He makes me lie down in green pastures.

He leads me beside still waters.

He restores my soul.

He leads me in paths of righteousness

for his name's sake.

Even though I walk through the valley
of the shadow of death,

I will fear no evil,

for you are with me;

your rod and your staff,

they comfort me.

You prepare a table before me

in the presence of my enemies;

you anoint my head with oil;

my cup overflows.

Surely goodness and mercy shall follow me
all the days of my life,

and I shall dwell in the house of
the Lord forever.

12

The Valley

DID THE PANDEMIC of 2020 cause you to think about your own mortality, about death itself? I am sure you felt heartbroken to hear of and see lifeless bodies by the dozens being kept in refrigerator trucks outside a hospital. The images forced us to think about death with a clarity and vulnerability most have never felt before. Did you think about your own death? The psalmist does.

The Bible does not shrink from showing us the reality of death. Every one of the characters in the Bible experienced death. No one gets out of life alive! (Okay, maybe Enoch did.) From the long list of burials in the book of our early ancestors in Genesis to the last pages of faithful followers of Jesus Christ in glory, everyone dies. Everyone is told early on, "Remember that you are dust and to dust you shall return."

The beauty of this poem is that it draws us into seeing an image of death we seldom contemplate. The Psalm tells us death is not the dark hole we may think it is. Death is not the one-way trip to the grave. Death is not a dead-end, as it were. With two separate words, the Psalm dispels our most pressing and depressing fears about our own death. Psalm 23 associates death with both a "valley" and a "shadow."

Death is like a valley. It is not a wall. It is not a pit. It is not a cliff. The good news about valleys is that they open up broadly into new lands. Valleys are a common feature of all beautiful landscapes; and they always lead somewhere. They always open up.

Further, imagine what our lives would be without any valleys. It would mean there is no mountain top. There is no summit. We would only live in the flatlands.

David was aware of death. He had seen it from the days of his youth. He had been hunted, as several attempts were made on his life. He lost a child to death. He would lose another. Yet he says that even in the middle of the valley of the shadow of death when the Lord is a Shepherd, He will lead His sheep through to the other side.

The only way out of death is through it. He will not fear because his Shepherd is there with him all the way.

Perhaps by now you are thinking more deeply about this Psalm than ever before. You now see why it has been read before, during, and after wars and battles and at hospital bedsides for generations. It speaks about the goodness of the Good Shepherd who will not leave His sheep, even in the valley.

When the Lord is my Shepherd,
I can go through the valley.

(When) The Lord is my shepherd; I shall not want.

He makes me lie down in green pastures.

He leads me beside still waters.

He restores my soul.

He leads me in paths of righteousness
for his name's sake.

Even though I walk through the valley
of the shadow of death,

I will fear no evil,

for you are with me;

your rod and your staff,

they comfort me.

You prepare a table before me

in the presence of my enemies;

you anoint my head with oil;

my cup overflows.

Surely goodness and mercy shall follow me
all the days of my life,

and I shall dwell in the house of
the Lord forever.

13

Valley of Death

WE DON'T LIKE TO THINK about death. When thoughts of death intrude on our lives, we don't want to dwell there. We turn our eyes away. But David doesn't turn away just yet. He describes death as a valley, meaning it is part of the landscape, a path we must pass through. He continues the metaphor, calling death a shadow—the "shadow of death."

In a way, we are always living in the shadow of death. Our death is a certainty. It is never about *if*, only *when*. W. H. Auden wrote that death is like the sound of distant thunder heard at a picnic. We know it is sure to come. This fact overshadows life. We all will get wet; we will all die sometime.

However, as we turn around and look at the shadow of death that follows us our entire lives, it turns out that it is pretty weak. Shadows are fragile. Any light that comes upon a shadow dispels it right away. It drives it back. Shadows evaporate in the presence of light. If you walk down a darkened hallway and open a door into a lighted room, the light scatters the darkness. The darkness does not flood into the light.

This is the New Testament in summary. Light is the antidote for the shadow of death.

The Bible shares three stories about Jesus coming into a gathering of people where someone has recently died: a 12-year-old girl, a young man, and Jesus' best friend, Lazarus. People are weeping and mourning. In every situation, because of Jesus' intervention, the dead person comes back to life. The weeping turns to cheering and celebration. The mourning for the dead turns to a joyful morning for the living! This is the effect light has upon darkness. It disperses it.

In Psalm 23, David is reminded of a time when he faced death himself. Whether in battle or when he was eluding Saul in the desert mountains, David knew the fear of the shadow of death. We do too. It has touched our families. It has come upon our loved ones. It is the thing we most fear for our children and their children. Yet it is the one thing that is common to all of us.

The Psalm says death, this omnipresent enemy follows us like a shadow. It will not go away, except in the light. But for now, in this life, under the shadow of our own death, we will never face it alone. David senses that, as often as he faced his own mortality, he always sensed the presence of the Lord as his Shepherd. There is great comfort then in knowing we will never face death alone.

The valley of the shadow of death is unavoidable. We will all be there one day. Maybe you feel you are near there now. Certainly, all of us are closer to it than we would like to think. But we can be assured that as the shadow of death will surround us one day, it cannot stand the power and presence of the Light.

When the Lord is my Shepherd, I know

that my death is not my final stop.

(When) The Lord is my shepherd; I shall not want.

He makes me lie down in green pastures.

He leads me beside still waters.

He restores my soul.

He leads me in paths of righteousness
for his name's sake.

Even though I walk through the valley
of the shadow of death,

I will fear no evil,

for you are with me;

your rod and your staff,

they comfort me.

You prepare a table before me

in the presence of my enemies;

you anoint my head with oil;

my cup overflows.

Surely goodness and mercy shall follow me
all the days of my life,

and I shall dwell in the house of
the Lord forever.

14

Fear No Evil

JOB IS NOT THE FIRST book in the Bible, but it is the first book *of* the Bible. It is the oldest book; it was written before the others. It focuses on the first issue that vexes most people: the problem of evil. Job asks repeatedly: *If God is good, why is there evil in the world?* It is a good question. It deserves a real answer. Unfortunately, the Book of Job doesn't really give the answer we want. It asks us to hold both of these truths as true at the same time: God is God, and God allows evil. (If you read the first chapter carefully you will see that God is allowing Satan to do evil. Satan is reporting back to God; God is in charge even when there is evil.)

You can hear the echo of Job in this line from Psalm 23. *I will fear no evil.* It does not say we will be protected from evil or buffered from its effects. None of us are immune to its consequences. There is evil in the world. It is all around us. The speaker isn't announcing he has an escape plan.

Instead, he says that in the face of evil he will have no fear. He will not be afraid. He will have (as we will see next) the presence and protection of God in his life all of his days. Jesus gave His followers the same comfort in John 16:33: "In this world you will have troubles, but fear not, I have overcome the world." We do not escape evil. Even still, we do not need to fear it.

As mentioned previously, David was no stranger to evil and violence. Some of it he caused; he committed notorious sins inflicting evil on others. But he was also a victim of it. Evil came after him. In Psalm 91 he references a plague that was stalking him; it was a 'wasting disease.' We do not know what it was, but these days everyone in the world can relate to the threat of a pandemic.

Our call to not fear evil is not a call to ignore it or to pretend it does not exist or affect us. But trusting the Shepherd means we are freed from a default response to evil—fight or flight. The fear of evil (in any form) is overcome by the presence of Christ.

David's poem shows that in his heart, he had no fear. Imagine that. No fear. Imagine being able to look at any evil that comes on you without fear. With Christ as Shepherd, we can face a disease that advances upon us, a financial failure that renders us vulnerable, or an experience that leaves us emotionally wounded. We can face these tragedies without fear.

How? How does this happen? Honestly, it cannot be measured or managed. It happens because Jesus said it would. In Mark 13 He tells His disciples that they need not fear what they would say if they were dragged before kings and magistrates and threatened. The Holy Spirit would be with them and tell them what to say. They would be empowered and sustained by the Holy Spirit of God.

After nearly 40 years of ordained ministry, I can say without hesitation that I have seen the power of God strengthen and uphold people as they faced unbelievable obstacles, even death. They were made strong to the end. The presence of the Holy Spirit was with them just as Jesus said He would be. The lack of fear is evidence of more than human bravery. It is a Divine presence. It is the 'presence' of our Triune God.

The more closely we follow our Good Shepherd, the more we trust Him and the less we fear evil. We see time and again how He guides, protects, and defends us day by day. This is the only way Christians through the ages have been able to face oppression, persecution, plagues, and even martyrdom. When the hour of need came, their Shepherd God was there with them to lead them through the valley without fear, just as David said He would.

When the Lord is my Shepherd,
I will have no fear.

(When) The Lord is my shepherd; I shall not want.

He makes me lie down in green pastures.

He leads me beside still waters.

He restores my soul.

He leads me in paths of righteousness
for his name's sake.

Even though I walk through the valley
of the shadow of death,

I will fear no evil,

for you are with me;

your rod and your staff,

they comfort me.

You prepare a table before me

in the presence of my enemies;

you anoint my head with oil;

my cup overflows.

Surely goodness and mercy shall follow me
all the days of my life,

and I shall dwell in the house of
the Lord forever.

15

With Me

"YOU ARE WITH ME," David says. The shepherd King knew more than most about the need for the presence of the Shepherd among the sheep. Here in the Psalm he strikes a bold note of confidence. *You are with me.* This short phrase might be the best way to sum up King David's faith. In the face of anything or everything, God is with him.

Did you notice that the 'voice' of the poem changes? With this phrase, David references God as 'you.' He is no longer relaying his beliefs *about* God. He is turning the Psalm God-ward, as it were, and addressing the Lord directly. David's song about God's character and generosity now becomes a hymn to a personal God.

The rest of the Psalm follows in this same voice. It is a beautiful transition. "You are with me."

We discussed the uniqueness of David's claim that God was *his* shepherd—that God is personal and knowable. The remarkable thing about a biblical faith is this stunning paradox. The Great and Cosmic God of the Universe, the Creator of all things visible and invisible, is also the God who has made Himself known to us. Consider the irony. He is beyond our imagination, but He is not beyond our reach. David's simple phrase means that God isn't just knowable; He can be palpable!

Psalm 23 is the most famous of the 150 psalms found in the Book of Psalms. But the Psalm just before it, Psalm 22, is the runner up. This Psalm was made famous by Jesus. He uttered it while on the cross. It's opening line is one of the seven last phrases that Jesus spoke as He died. "My God, my God, why have you forsaken me?" This Psalm is so associated with Jesus that it is hard to remember that these words came from King David. Surely David felt abandoned by God. We all have. But the end of Psalm 22 is as optimistic and positive as one could imagine. Weeping and grief are all human and normal reactions to the hard things we have to face. But in the end, God's presence can be felt. It is, as I say, palpable.

"God is with me." This phrase is a good candidate for your elevator speech about what Christians believe. Let's say you are standing in an elevator going up to the third floor of a building. The door opens on the second floor and a stranger enters and presses number 4. He sees you have a cross on the lapel of your sports coat. It is just the two of you. Then he says, "You are wearing a cross on your jacket. I have always wanted to ask a Christian a simple question." He pauses as the elevator door closes and the car begins to ascend slowly. He continues. "So, let me ask you, as a Christian what do you truly believe?"

You have 10 seconds.

What do you say? I don't recommend a fast version of The Nicene Creed. Your testimony is probably too long too. What about David's claim that God is with him? Why not say, "I believe that through Jesus Christ, I am never alone."

The chime dings and the metal doors open slowly. As you leave the elevator car you say, "In other words, God is always with me, and thanks for asking."

The Apostle Paul writes the same thing most memorably at the end of Romans, Chapter 8. He writes "neither death nor life, nor angels nor rulers, nor things present nor things to come, nor powers, nor height nor depth, nor anything else in all creation, will be able to separate us from the love of God in Christ Jesus our Lord."

God is always with us. This is David's bold statement.

When the Lord is my Shepherd,
I know I am never alone.

(When) The Lord is my shepherd; I shall not want.

He makes me lie down in green pastures.

He leads me beside still waters.

He restores my soul.

He leads me in paths of righteousness

for his name's sake.

Even though I walk through the valley
of the shadow of death,

I will fear no evil,

for you are with me;

your rod and your staff,

they comfort me.

You prepare a table before me

in the presence of my enemies;

you anoint my head with oil;

my cup overflows.

Surely goodness and mercy shall follow me
all the days of my life,

and I shall dwell in the house of
the Lord forever.

16

Rod and Staff

PSALM 23 WAS WRITTEN nearly 1000 years before the birth of our Lord. It has been easy to understand the meaning of this great poem so far. But we are about to move into an area of the poem that will need more explanation. What would have been plain to David will be opaque to us today unless we take the time to define some terms.

The word *rod* refers to a large sturdy stick about the size of a walking cane. It was, along with the staff, a shepherd's tool. In the evening, when the shepherd would begin to bring his sheep into a makeshift sheep pen, he would stand at the gate of the pen and put his rod across the entrance. Then one by one, sheep by sheep, the shepherd would let them into the secure site. The rod was used to count off the sheep one by one and prod or push them into safety for the night.

We are much more familiar with the word *staff*. This was a second instrument that was used by the shepherd. This staff, longer than the rod, might have had a hook on its end, and it was used to guide the sheep in the right direction. It was also used to rescue sheep from the dangerous places they might wander.

In short, the rod prods and pushes sheep where they may never want to go. The staff pulls sheep back from where they might wrongly want to go. One pushes. The other pulls.

Why does David call this pushing and pulling a source of comfort? These instruments seem like annoying ways of prodding or controlling the sheep. We don't like it when people (or God) tell us what to do, where to go, and where not to go. We shirk off this kind of interference. But for David, it is a source of comfort.

Consider, though, how often we have been forced to go somewhere we didn't want to go, only to realize it was precisely where we were meant to be. And who has not had the experience of having been pulled from the brink of destruction when we followed what we felt so certain was good for us?

We need the rod and we need the staff. Uncomfortable as the prodding and nudging may be, they soon become a comfort. They remind us that when the Lord is our Shepherd, there is someone to save us from ourselves.

That is why our daily prayer always includes a confession of sin. Why? Because we need the daily reminder that, left to our own judgment, we'll never make it safely into the pen, and we will probably choose to wander right into a wolf's den.

If we want to call the Lord our Shepherd we should also be guided, comforted, and even corrected by His loving hand. Remember the way the writer of Hebrews puts it: "My son, do not regard lightly the discipline of the Lord, nor be weary when reproved by him. For the Lord disciplines the one he loves" (Hebrews 12:5-6). There were times when the Lord truly did discipline David with a rod. His sin with Bathsheba was a terrible chapter in his life. Uriah, Bathsheba's husband, and David's good friend was intentionally killed in battle. Their love child would sicken and die. When David repents of this sin, he repents as a broken man before

God (Psalm 51). He was thoroughly chastened. As he confessed his sin, he also confessed his love of God.

David surely could tell us of the times he almost 'went there,' almost fell into sin, but because of the remembrance of God's love, or the presence of His 'hook', David was protected.

We know that God is with us, that He is *for* us, because we feel the brunt of His direction and discipline, protecting us, even from ourselves.

When the Lord is my Shepherd,
I will be comforted by God's correction.

(When) The Lord is my shepherd; I shall not want.

He makes me lie down in green pastures.

He leads me beside still waters.

He restores my soul.

He leads me in paths of righteousness
for his name's sake.

Even though I walk through the valley
of the shadow of death,

I will fear no evil,

for you are with me;

your rod and your staff,

they comfort me.

You prepare a table before me

in the presence of my enemies;

you anoint my head with oil;

my cup overflows.

Surely goodness and mercy shall follow me
all the days of my life,

and I shall dwell in the house of
the Lord forever.

17

Enemies

ONE OF THE MANDATES that every Christian is charged to follow is to pray for our enemies. Jesus spoke these words, "But I tell you, love your enemies, bless those who curse you, do good to those who hate you, and pray for those who mistreat you and persecute you." Jesus modeled this in His own life. The early church undoubtedly prayed for their enemies. They had many enemies. And, as they prayed for their enemies, God changed their hearts *and* sometimes the hearts of their enemies.

Consider the Apostle Paul. Before his conversion, he was an enemy of the church. Today we would use the word 'terrorist' to describe Paul. He punished people for their faith in Jesus. He was a zealot for religious purity. He approved of a mob murder of the church's first martyr Stephen. How did a man like this become the greatest missionary the church has ever seen?

Prayer. Nothing else would explain the radical and complete change of heart of this particular man. The Damascus Road experience was the place of conversion, high noon was the time of the conversion. But it seems that prayer was the cause of his conversion.

David does not know this command to pray for one's enemies 1,000 years before Christ. He is a man of his own time. He knows that a warrior kills his enemies. He plunders their cities, enslaves their women, and kills every man on the other side. It is the law. It is '*lex talionis*', the law of retribution. It was practiced widely in the ancient world. It would have been the standard method of operation for the armies of Israel under David's command.

As the Shepherd has been with the sheep through the most difficult days of his life, in the Valley of the Shadow of death, David emerges on the other side. In the Psalm, he finds that a table has been set for a feast, and the feasting begins.

This is where there might be a glimmer of hope for humanity. In the Psalm, David's enemies have not been executed. David is no longer threatened by them. They are there in his presence as he feasts with God at the banqueting table.

During the Civil War, Abraham Lincoln made a speech in which he expressed sympathy for the citizen rebels in the South. He was promptly skewered by someone in the audience. If the goal of the war is to destroy the enemy, why was the President soft on them. His answer is classic and true. He said, "Madam, I destroy my enemies when I make them my friends?"

This is hard to do. Sometimes it is impractical. Sometimes it is impossible. Praying for one's enemies and NOT extinguishing them is one of the core values of the Christian faith.

Paul, who is Exhibit A of what happens when Christians pray, had a difficult time letting go of his anger and forgiving his own enemies. Yet in his last letter to young Timothy, he warns Timothy about turning his enemies over for God to judge.

This is how we should deal with our enemies. We cannot eliminate them. Sometimes we may not be able to make them friends, but we can turn them over into the hands of our God.

When the Lord is my Shepherd,

I can turn my enemies over to God.

(When) The Lord is my shepherd; I shall not want.

He makes me lie down in green pastures.

He leads me beside still waters.

He restores my soul.

He leads me in paths of righteousness
for his name's sake.

Even though I walk through the valley
of the shadow of death,

I will fear no evil,

for you are with me;

your rod and your staff,

they comfort me.

You prepare a table before me

in the presence of my enemies;

you anoint my head with oil;

my cup overflows.

Surely goodness and mercy shall follow me
all the days of my life,

and I shall dwell in the house of
the Lord forever.

18

A Table in the Wilderness

SUDDENLY, DAVID has changed the 'voice' of the psalm, as we noted before. He moves from talking about the Lord as Shepherd to speaking to Him as a friend and companion. He uses '*You*' instead of '*He*'. In the first part of the psalm, David is like a sheep and the Lord is the shepherd. That relationship is one-sided. The Shepherd is the dominant presence over the sheep; he looks down over the sheep and the sheep look up at the shepherd. But when David switches the 'voice' of the psalm to the more familiar 'you', the relationship changes. It is as if the two have become friends.

Here the Psalm's imagery switches from pastoral shepherd caring for the sheep to one of even greater intimacy. The narrator is a man and the Lord is a friend, an intimate friend who provides for David. David has gone *through* the valley of the shadow of death. Because of the Shepherd, he does not fear. As he emerges from this valley he has not only endured, but he has triumphed. In order to celebrate this triumph, the Lord has set up a table in the wilderness in the very presence of the people who were once a threat.

This is a remarkable idea! It shows us that no one is immune from the suffering of life, especially near the end of our natural life. But not only is the presence of the Lord with us, there is the promise of a new life beyond. This is what the Apostle Paul captured in his letter to the Corinthians: *For these light and momentary troubles are nothing in comparison to the eternal glory that awaits us. (2 Corinthians 4:7)*

Believers in God have a different understanding of trauma and hardships. Some people use the evils of the day to try to prove that there is no God; that there are random acts of terror, violence, assault, and evil mayhem that come and go without any order or cause. But anyone who has faith in a personal God—a God who is both shepherd and friend—will say something different. They will say that the hardships in their lives actually proved God was real. He was there before the hard times and He gave strength to endure what was next. At the end of the difficulties, He was nearer to us (and we to Him) than we could have ever imagined.

Again, this same idea was given by Paul in Romans 8:37: "…in all these things we are more than conquerors through him who loved us." I have always loved the phrase "more than conquerors." It means that in our lives, we are not just about enduring problems or getting through challenges. That is only about surviving. The Psalm takes us to a new understanding of victory. With the presence of the Lord in our lives, as He guides, protects, and defends us, we thrive.

We come to a better place on the other side.

Psalm 23 tells us simply that the only way out of hard times is to go *through* the hard times. At the end of the hardest of times, the Lord who went through our pain with us as a shepherd is waiting for us on the other side as a friend.

When the Lord is my Shepherd,
I will see the Lord as my friend.

(When) The Lord is my shepherd; I shall not want.

He makes me lie down in green pastures.

He leads me beside still waters.

He restores my soul.

He leads me in paths of righteousness
for his name's sake.

Even though I walk through the valley
of the shadow of death,

I will fear no evil,

for you are with me;

your rod and your staff,

they comfort me.

You prepare a table before me

in the presence of my enemies;

you anoint my head with oil;

my cup overflows.

Surely goodness and mercy shall follow me
all the days of my life,

and I shall dwell in the house of
the Lord forever.

19

Anointed Head

SOME PEOPLE READ the psalm a bit differently at this point in the text. They imagine that the anointing mentioned here is performed as it was practiced in the field, to salve any sores or wounds. That is, the psalmist is still using the sheep/shepherd metaphor, imagining himself as a sheep and the Lord as his Shepherd. This is a common and popular reading of the 23rd Psalm.

But as I have read it over and over again, I see something else. I hear a change in tone and voice as mentioned above. The image of a sheep transforms into an image of a man, a friend. This makes the anointing moment even more rich and wonderful. Let me explain.

In the ancient world, being invited to share a meal with someone was a rare honor. It was an invitation to enter into a deeper relationship. It was the seal of a friendship. And here, there are clear and vivid indications that a solid relationship between the Lord and the poet has been sealed.

First, there is a well-set table in the presence of the defeated enemies. In this, the Lord allowed David to survive an ordeal. But those terrors and fears of people or places can never do any more harm. The Psalm tells us that a victory party is set up for us on the other side of our journey. The feast is hosted by our friend, the Lord. The table is set for a banquet like none other. To show the overwhelming victory, the banquet table is surrounded by our enemies who are not invited! As mentioned above, in this way we are more than conquerors.

This is not just any feast. In fact, as I read it, it sounds more like a wedding feast; the kind that Jesus visited in John 2. To eat at a table, to drink from overflowing cups of wine, and to anoint one's head with oil is, in fact, the imagery of a truly deep relationship. I suggest that it might be related to a marriage feast because of the way the image ends. David is invited not only to eat and drink and be anointed, but He is promised that he will dwell in the house of the Lord forever. That is a marriage.

But in any case, we have two images in the poem that need to be unpacked for our modern ears and minds. What is anointing and what is an overflowing cup?

The anointing of the head with oil was done on occasions when the host wanted the person to be honored or made special in the sight of everyone. Readers of the New Testament will remember that Jesus was anointed with oil by a woman in the home of a Pharisee. This act of love prompted the Lord to forgive this sinful woman of her many offenses. It also caused Him to rebuke the owner of the house for not honoring the one who could forgive sins.

The point is that anointing of the head with oil is not a throw-away image. It is proof that there is a special connection between the host and the guest. But most remarkable here is that the Lord is the one who is anointing David. It is His table. It is His feast. It is His party. It is His overflowing cup. It is the Lord who has acted upon the poet. David is the guest. He is the recipient of all the blessings, even to the point of having a cup of wine that is overflowing.

Religion is a common human enterprise. We see primitive and sophisticated forms of religion all over the globe in all kinds of circumstances. Regardless of their differences in ethics or beliefs, they all share a common feature. They are all about humanity's attempts to reach an unseen God. One aspect of religion is to answer the human desire to do things that will add years, even eternal years, to our lives.

Christianity, in this sense, is not a religion at all. Its strength does not depend on what we can do to reach God. As God provides the table, the oil, and the wine, Christianity is the recognition that God has provided EVERYTHING we need.

We do not need to try to reach God. In Christ, God has reached us. He has come into our world to save sinners.

When the Lord is my Shepherd,
I know God blesses me.

(When) The Lord is my shepherd; I shall not want.

He makes me lie down in green pastures.

He leads me beside still waters.

He restores my soul.

He leads me in paths of righteousness
for his name's sake.

Even though I walk through the valley
of the shadow of death,

I will fear no evil,

for you are with me;

your rod and your staff,

they comfort me.

You prepare a table before me

in the presence of my enemies;

you anoint my head with oil;

my cup overflows.

Surely goodness and mercy shall follow me
all the days of my life,

and I shall dwell in the house of
the Lord forever.

20

Overflowing

THE SECOND IMAGE in this verse is an overflowing cup. This is not hard to understand. The cup is filled with good wine and the good wine is overflowing. Obviously, the celebration will last a long time and the wine will be poured freely. Is the Bible endorsing binge drinking? Not at all. The Psalm is showing us what is waiting for all who come out of the valley to find the table our gracious Host and Friend has set.

The Psalm is telling us that the life to come is a glorious celebration where there is no end. The image of the overflowing cup, in the language of the Bible, refers to the lavish abundance and generosity of God. This is a foreshadowing of Jesus' first miracle in Cana of Galilee when the best wine started overflowing for all the guests.

Do you remember the scene we mentioned earlier from John 7 when Jesus cries out for anyone who is thirsty to come to him? He meant it. He promised if anyone came to Him and began to drink the water He gave, springs of water would well up. It would begin to overflow. This is David's point. In the presence of his God, seated and feasting, his cup is overflowing. There is no end to the joy being poured out for everyone!

Taken alongside the anointing of his head, David experiences the grace of God and the generosity of God. This is extravagant, wonderful, outrageously generous, lavish love. Not only is it unexpected; it is also undeserved.

This world-altering love is described most powerfully in Jesus' most famous Parable of the Prodigal Son in Luke 15. Consider the perspectives of each of the three figures in the story: The Rebel Son, The Elder Brother, and the Forgiving Father.

The younger brother expects that his abject rebellion has damaged his relationship with the family. He knows, as we all would, that something within the bonds of family love has been broken; he knows it can't be fixed. He will never be his father's son again after the selfish things he has done. He hopes that his father might allow him a servant's role apart from the comforts of the family.

The older brother expects that justice will be served. His younger brother wasted the family fortune. He broke his father's heart. He dishonored the family name. There are debts to the family that must be paid. Justice should be meted out harshly.

But the father does not condemn the boy. The father opens his heart to his son. The father embraces the son and restores the son back into his place in the family. The father isn't naïve about the shame caused by the son. He isn't bad at accounting; he knows that the losses are real. His pain is real. But none of that matters as he looks for his son, still far away, coming home. The love he feels for his son overwhelms everything else.

This will never make sense to our impoverished imaginations. Our cups seldom, if ever, overflow. But God's generosity and grace are relentless and inexhaustible. God is not diminished by giving so freely to us. It only expands His glory.

One great scene from the New Testament will prove the point. Peter was a good businessman but a bad fisherman. In several stories in the Gospels, he comes home with empty nets.

One morning, as Peter was washing his unlucky nets, Jesus tells him to give fishing one more try. Peter reluctantly agrees. He casts the nets where he is told, and a massive catch of fish is drawn up out of the water. There are more fish than he had ever imagined. The scene turns chaotic as the nets are filled to overflowing. Peter admits to the Lord that this catch was far more than could ever deserve. His sin made him feel unworthy of the Lord's miraculous generosity.

God's generous love is always overflowing.

When the Lord is my Shepherd,
I know his never-ending generosity
and grace.

(When) The Lord is my shepherd; I shall not want.

He makes me lie down in green pastures.

He leads me beside still waters.

He restores my soul.

He leads me in paths of righteousness
for his name's sake.

Even though I walk through the valley
of the shadow of death,

I will fear no evil,

for you are with me;

your rod and your staff,

they comfort me.

You prepare a table before me

in the presence of my enemies;

you anoint my head with oil;

my cup overflows.

Surely goodness and mercy shall follow me
all the days of my life,

and I shall dwell in the house of
the Lord forever.

21

Goodness and Mercy

IN THIS PART OF THE POEM we are told that there are two gifts given to David by his Friend. He has been through the Valley. He has come out on the other side. He has feasted in the wilderness. He has such a decisive victory that he can feast confidently while all of his enemies surround him. He has been anointed with oil. Great wine is freely poured. Based on all of these riches that are now his, he is assured that the rest of his life will be followed by the goodness and mercy of God.

What a remarkable statement from David, given that he wrote it 1,000 years before Christ. This is a hint, a foreshadowing of the Gospel itself.

Consider the meaning of the words goodness and mercy. Goodness is giving a person (such as my sinful self) what they do not deserve. None of us, because of our sin and rebellious nature, deserve God's goodness. David knew this about his own life. He knew he was a dedicated sinner who deserved to be punished. Yet, God gave him what he did not deserve. The Bible's word for this goodness is *grace*.

Mercy is the opposite. Mercy is when God does NOT give us what we DO deserve. Mercy is not about withholding judgment; it is about witholding the punishment. David knew this much about himself. He deserved punishment for his sins. I know it about myself. Undoubtedly you know this about yourself, too, and so does God. He knows what we deserve. But instead, He grants us mercy.

Indeed, the New Testament talks about the gifts of goodness and mercy in the familiar words of 'grace' and 'mercy'. In the mind of the Apostle Paul, these are two sides of the same coin, and the coin is love. This love will follow us day by day for the rest of our lives.

God's love is not theoretical. It is never detached from our human experience and how we face the challenges of our day. God's love can always be described in the language of the New Testament as both *grace* (giving us what is not deserved) and *mercy* (not giving us what is deserved). When a person comes to faith in Christ, they receive these gifts as a matching set, the goodness of God and the mercy of God. Glory to God!

This closing statement in the Psalm underscores what we have heard throughout. The promise isn't just for now—it's for all our days.

When the Lord is my Shepherd,
I receive God's goodness and mercy
all of my days.

(When) The Lord is my shepherd; I shall not want.

He makes me lie down in green pastures.

He leads me beside still waters.

He restores my soul.

He leads me in paths of righteousness
for his name's sake.

Even though I walk through the valley
of the shadow of death,

I will fear no evil,

for you are with me;

your rod and your staff,

they comfort me.

You prepare a table before me

in the presence of my enemies;

you anoint my head with oil;

my cup overflows.

Surely goodness and mercy shall follow me
all the days of my life,

and I shall dwell in the house of
the Lord forever.

22

The Days of my Life

DAVID'S LIFE WAS LONG and eventful. It was filled with color, conviction, and compromise at many turns. We are told that he was a man after God's own heart. This means that he loved the heart of God and he tried to model his life after it. He was successful at this some of the time. Sadly, he was not successful all of the time.

Consider the five different ages or periods of David's life.

The Quiet Years: From birth to about 17 years old. His early role was as the family shepherd in the field. While not all of the psalms are written by King David, scholars believe that many of his own psalms emerged from these years of backwoods solitude.

The Strong Years: From 17-22 years old. In these years he is 'discovered' by Samuel and chosen as the next king. He emerges into public life with major victories as a warrior and gains national prominence for killing Goliath.

The Exile Years: From 23-31. David marries the King's daughter, Michal, but the family later breaks down and Saul hunts David for seven years in the wilderness. Undoubtedly many Psalms were written over the angst and pain of these years.

The Ruling Years: From 32 to 70. These are the years of David's reign as King. His reign is marked by major victories, national pride, personal failures, family disintegration, and tears.

The End Years: From 70+. He is revered in his final years. He has outgrown his personal excesses, dies a national hero in 970 BCE, and, as the Bible has it, is 'gathered to his fathers'. He leaves Solomon as King and directs him to fulfill a few final vendettas.

David's life had been full of promise and hope in the early years. The reputation he gained for military strength and courage and spiritual love of God made him one of the favorite kings of all time. He succeeded in big ways and the people cheered. His failures were epic, and the people suffered.

He may be seen as the consummate human: real, ideal, but with large feet of clay. He is every man and an aspect of all of humanity. This is why Renaissance master Michelangelo chose David as a young, virile, heroic man to display his glory as an aspect of all humanity. Today "The David" is in Florence, Italy. He is tall, relaxed, confident, and he stands victorious over Goliath. The statue of the young man at age 17 is 17 feet tall, naked, and unashamed.

King David died at age 72. He would hardly have made a model human being then. He could not keep warm. His hormones and excesses had ceased, but hatred for some of his enemies remains.

Those are 'all his days'.

This is the claim of the Bible. No matter how high we go or how far we fall, no matter how rough we've had it or how rough we've made it for others, God's gifts of goodness and mercy are always following us. They pursue us. In Christ, they are freely offered. They come with knowing the Lord Jesus. Sometimes we welcome them, and our lives flourish. Sadly, sometimes we reject them both and bring pain down upon ourselves.

When the Lord is my Shepherd,
I can trust Him all the days of my life.

(When) The Lord is my shepherd; I shall not want.

He makes me lie down in green pastures.

He leads me beside still waters.

He restores my soul.

He leads me in paths of righteousness
for his name's sake.

Even though I walk through the valley
of the shadow of death,

I will fear no evil,

for you are with me;

your rod and your staff,

they comfort me.

You prepare a table before me

in the presence of my enemies;

you anoint my head with oil;

my cup overflows.

Surely goodness and mercy shall follow me
all the days of my life,

and I shall dwell in the house of
the Lord forever.

23

Dwelling Forever

THE PANDEMIC OF 2020 has made many realize just how vulnerable we are to death, and how short life really is. Given the expanse of time in the universe and the scant years of recorded history, our life is, as the Bible says, a breath. But even more sobering is that it is a short breath that fades quickly.

Death ultimately touches every person on the planet and most people have always wanted to have an answer to the question, "What happens when we die?" Religions and philosophies have never settled this existential question.

But the Christian faith reframes the question completely. Instead of asking "What happens when we die?" the New Testament asks, "What if death is not supposed to be our final outcome?" In other words, what if we are made for a different kind of life? What if we were made to honor and glorify God forever, but our world went sideways and one day it will be made right again?

I often think this way when I am asked to officiate at a formal memorial service or liturgy. I have presided over hundreds of them for people who were advanced in years and for those who are tragically young. I always sense a very unsettling question that is seldom answered at funerals: "Where did she go?"

For every funeral, I prepare a full sermon. On one particular occasion, for the service of a brilliant woman I had known for many years, I found myself wandering far from my notes. I began to wonder out loud what happened to this magnificent life force that gave so much to so many. I asked, "How can someone like this just..." I paused for a moment to be sure I had the right word. I did. I ended that sentence with the word "end." *How can someone like this just end?*

If we read the Bible carefully, it seems we are designed for a very different kind of life than the one we live. The Bible tells the truth that we are dust and to dust we will return. But that is the outward form. The hope of the Bible is that life never ends; it is only changed. The only proof we have of this truth is the resurrection of Jesus Christ. That is why Paul says that if the resurrection of

Christ is false, we Christians, among all people, are to be pitied the most.

As Psalm 23 concludes, David tells us that the final hope he has is this biblical hope. He will dwell in the house of the Lord. . . . forever. There is no end to forever.

It is forever and ever. David's sincere faith allowed him to see the Lord as first his Shepherd (verses 1-3) and then his Friend (verses 4-5) and then finally as his Eternal Head of Household.

When the Lord is my Shepherd,
my eternity is with Him.

When
THE LORD IS
MY SHEPHERD

PSALM 23 IS one of the most cherished Psalms in the world. Now that we have finished the journey through it, I hope you can see why. It holds wonderful and enduring images available to any reader in any circumstance. It offers hidden treasures buried deep beneath the surface. As we have seen, when we take one word or one idea and look closely, new things emerge that show us the love of God and His care for us.

This is the value of going through the Psalm slowly. We call it "the Word of God" for good reason. It speaks to us in every word. God's chosen means to communicate His will and show His glory are found in the language, images, metaphors, and ideas of the Bible.

Our faith in God is meant to be more than religious. As we have seen, religion is usually understood as a prescribed set of human practices and doctrines that are observed to help a person *reach* God. They are human activities intended to bring people closer to God. These actions and practices help the religion, the faith, what we might think of as the church, guide us day by day. They help us transmit faith to our children so they can draw closer to God. This is the religious part of the way we take hold of the faith.

But drawing close to God is only one aspect of living a faithful life. The other is knowing how He draws close to us. This is personal to us. It is close to our hearts.

I hope that this familiar Psalm was renewed and refreshed for you by the addition of a single word, "*When*." That one word makes the beautiful images and ideas that occurred to David 3,000 years ago take aim directly into our lives. They become promises. We say "'When' the Lord is my Shepherd…" and claim all those promises as our own. That is not simply a religion; it is a deeply personal relationship.

So, what will it mean for you to embrace these promises right now?

The Pandemic of 2020 was as sudden as it was tragic. There was virtually no time to prepare our lives and our families for it. We were caught flat-footed. Have you seen how quickly people in your community joined the thousands in line at the local food bank? Have you seen how many businesses have shuttered their doors? Many of them will not come back. These are massive losses on very personal levels. Everyone is impacted. Everyone.

There are many questions facing us right now, but I believe there is one question that needs an answer from each of us. It is the first question we must answer and it is the one of greatest importance.

Is the Lord your Shepherd?

I invite you to answer this question today. Is the Lord your Shepherd? Make this your personal, prayerful confession of faith every day. Say, "When the Lord is my Shepherd" as you begin your day in the morning and end it at night. See what happens.

You may find all your *wants* fading away. You may feel secure enough to set aside your constant worry and lie down in God's pasture. You may sense your wearied, worn-out, sinful soul is being restored. You may find, after all your wandering, a path that leads you to righteousness, back to a right relationship with God. You may discover the lurking fear of death that haunts you is only a valley leading out to a new and better place, a shadow the light will cast out. You may find that while evil still surrounds you (it will never go away), you are no longer paralyzed by fear, because God is with you. You may feel the *comfort* of His rod and staff, nudging you back to the way. Even more, you may find your hope renewed that one day you will come to a table set before you in the house of your great Host and Friend, where you will dwell forever and ever.

When we look at our problems and challenges, we are either going to face them with the Lord as our Shepherd, or we will face them alone. Daily confess your need for the Shepherd. He has promised to be with you.

You can make your commitment clear today. Write your name and today's date on the line below confirming your faith in the Lord as your Shepherd and your desire to follow where He leads. All the goodness and mercy that God has for you will follow you all the days of your life, when the Lord is your Shepherd.

Name:

Date:

1
ACKNOWLEDGMENTS

I HAVE COME TO SEE that writing is both a privilege and burden that I could never carry without the encouragement and support of my wife, Fran. Years ago, she helped me see that the Scriptures of the Old and New Testament could be seen not only as the Word of God, but as the Artwork of God. I am thankful to God for all the insight and beauty Fran has brought into my life.

I have been working with a colleague of mine from my days as Rector of Christ Church. Daniel Adkinson is a great conversation partner who helped me refine the early manuscript of this book. I have also come to know Bruce Barbour and Karen Moore. They are a power couple when it comes to writing and publishing. Our friendship has been forged over video conferences only; we have actually never met. We hope to change that soon.

Early readers of this manuscript will find that nearly all of their helpful suggestions and edits were fully incorporated into the final edition. Thank you, Al, John, Christie, Jane, Karen and Bruce. What a blessing to have your input and encouraging words.

I am thankful to God for showing me more about Himself in David's 3,000-year-old psalm than I had ever imagined. I am even more thankful for the love, care, guidance and, presence of Jesus Christ in my life. He is the Good Shepherd. The Lord has saved me and He guides me all the days of my life.

DAVID ROSEBERRY is an ordained Anglican priest and has been in ministry for nearly 40 years. He was founding Rector of Christ Church in Plano for over 30 years and now is the founding director of LeaderWorks, a non-profit ministry that serves churches and church leaders. He is a speaker, writer, teacher, and minister at large for the Anglican Church in North America. David Roseberry lives north of Dallas with his wife, Fran.

When the Lord is My Shepherd is his third book.

Made in the USA
Coppell, TX
15 December 2020

45062762R00090